Original title:
Shattered Stillness

Copyright © 2024 Creative Arts Management OÜ
All rights reserved.

Author: William Hawthorne
ISBN HARDBACK: 978-9916-90-722-1
ISBN PAPERBACK: 978-9916-90-723-8

The Quiet After the Crack

In shadows cast by fading light,
Whispers linger, soft and slight.
A world held breath, a hush profound,
In silence, broken dreams resound.

The echoes of a shattering sound,
As memories drift, lost and found.
Hearts mend slowly, stitch by stitch,
In the calm, they find their niche.

Fractured Peace

A fragile calm on shattered ground,
Where every heartbeat makes a sound.
The pieces lie, both near and far,
Beneath the weight of each fallen star.

Whispers rise like chilled night air,
As dreams unfold in silent prayer.
Yet hope entwines with threads of pain,
In fractured peace, we start again.

When Silence Breaks

In stillness, shadows start to move,
A gentle nudge, a heartbeat proves.
Voices tremble in the dark,
Each fleeting thought, a silent spark.

The hush once warm begins to shift,
Unraveling, as hearts uplift.
A sudden storm of sound returns,
From silence, life itself now burns.

Chunks of a Silent Soul

Fragments lost in quiet layers,
Stories told through distant prayers.
In every piece, a tale of woe,
A silent song that yearns to grow.

Shattered dreams and whispered screams,
Collecting hope in fragile beams.
Each chunk, a treasure buried deep,
A silent soul that longs to leap.

Cracked Reflections of Light

In the glass of shattered dreams,
Shadows dance with silent screams.
Colors bleed in fractured hues,
Mirrors hold forgotten news.

Flickering flames of fleeting time,
Resounding echoes of a rhyme.
Every shard a story told,
A world of whispers, bright and bold.

The Breakage of Calm Waters

Beneath the surface, silence sleeps,
A gentle hush before it weeps.
Ripples spread with every thought,
In reflections, battles fought.

A stone disturbs the tranquil scene,
Creating chaos where it's been.
Stillness shatters, truths collide,
Emotions rushing like the tide.

Tides of Unspoken Word

In the depths of quiet seas,
Words are lost on whispering breeze.
Secrets linger close to shore,
Yearning to be heard, to soar.

Currents pull, the heartstrings play,
A melody that fades away.
Promises held in silent night,
Awaiting dawn to bring them light.

Silent Echoes of Disarray

In the chaos, silence reigns,
An orchestra of hidden pains.
Voices lost in tangled threads,
Invisible paths where hope treads.

A symphony of uncried tears,
Resonates within the fears.
Echoes whisper, shadows sway,
In this dance of disarray.

The Silence Between Cracks

In shadows where whispers still flow,
A world hides in the softest glow.
Glimmers of peace, caught in the air,
Echoes of dreams that linger and stare.

Between the moments, a sigh remains,
Gentle touch of invisible chains.
Each crack a story, each silence a song,
Threads of existence where we all belong.

Fraying Threads of Quiet

In the corners where stillness resides,
Fraying threads weave the truth that hides.
Each heartbeat a pulse of fragile time,
In quiet places, chaos can chime.

The tapestry frays, but still we hold tight,
In the tapestry woven with soft moonlight.
Moments unravel, yet beauty is found,
In whispers of love, where silence is crowned.

When Tranquility Splinters

A soft crack appears in the calm veneer,
Ripples cascade as the echoes draw near.
Fractured reflections in pools of the past,
Moments of stillness, too fleeting to last.

The gentle facade begins to distort,
In realms of the quiet, shadows cavort.
When peace is shattered, new rhythms will rise,
In chaos we find the strength to be wise.

Echoes of a Broken Calm

Beyond the stillness where echoes now play,
A symphony lingers, both soft and gray.
Every sharp breath reveals hidden strife,
In the layers of silence, layers of life.

The calm may be broken, yet hope will ignite,
An ember of courage that sparks the night.
In the dance of despair, the heart finds its way,
Through echoes of calm that never decay.

After the Quiet Storm

Whispers of the wind arise,
Leaves dance softly, touch the skies.
The echoes fade into the night,
As stars emerge, a gentle light.

Calm settles over the weary ground,
Nature's breath, a soothing sound.
The world transforms, anew it seems,
Awakening from restless dreams.

Clouds drift away on silver streams,
In twilight's glow, our hope redeems.
Together we embrace the peace,
As every worry starts to cease.

So let us bask in softest light,
After the storm, peace takes flight.
In tender hues, the world will sigh,
And in its warmth, our hearts will lie.

Pieces of a Broken Dawn

Fragments scatter in the light,
Colors blend where shadows fight.
The sky is torn, yet strangely whole,
As daybreak whispers to the soul.

With each ray, a story wakes,
From shattered dreams, new hope takes.
The heart learns to mend in gray,
Finding strength in a new day.

Silhouettes of night retreat,
Lessons learned in bitter sweet.
Distant echoes, soft and warm,
Embrace the pieces of the dawn.

These moments fragile, yet they shine,
In fleeting beauty, we define.
A palette rich with hues undone,
We gather hope 'til we're all one.

Fragments of an Untold Story

In corners dim where shadows dwell,
Lie forgotten dreams, a silent spell.
Whispers linger, tales unsaid,
In pages worn, a life we led.

The ink of time leaves marks unseen,
Moments cherished, lost between.
A glance, a smile, a secret shared,
The heart remembers, always bared.

In meadows green where children played,
Ghosts of laughter, memories made.
We stitch the past with threads of gold,
In every story, love unfolds.

Yet fragments scatter like the breeze,
Fading softly through the trees.
An untold tale, just out of reach,
In every silence, lessons teach.

Dissonance in Daydreams

Colors clash in restless minds,
A symphony of tangled finds.
Lost in thoughts, we skirmish wide,
In daydreams where the shadows bide.

Laughter echoes, a haunting tune,
Beneath the glow of a questioning moon.
Softly swirling, chaos reigns,
In every beat, a heart contains.

We wander through the tangled lore,
Embracing truths we can't ignore.
Waves of doubt and vivid light,
Dance together, ignite the night.

In dissonance, we find our grace,
A bittersweet, enduring space.
For in the clash, our spirits soar,
Creating music forevermore.

The Fraying Edge of Quiet

In the stillness, whispers fade,
Shadows dance, softly swayed.
Echoes linger, haunting peace,
Threads unravel, never cease.

Silence trembles, heartbeats race,
A fragile world, in its place.
Faintest sounds of distant lands,
Slip through grasping, nervous hands.

Ripples in the Tranquil

Gentle waves on glassy lakes,
Beneath the surface, change awakes.
A pebble tossed, a breath of air,
Transforms the calm with tender care.

Still reflections break apart,
Painting stories, art by heart.
Ripples spread, a dance of fate,
Softly urging us to wait.

Moments of Broken Serenity

Stillness shattered, echoes flare,
Quiet corners, stripped laid bare.
A glance exchanged, a fleeting sigh,
Moments lost, yet never die.

In between the peace and storm,
A fragile heart begins to warm.
Broken pieces, slight repair,
Whispers cling, as we lay bare.

Whispered Cracks in Time

Time slips through like soft-spun thread,
Leaves us pondering what lies ahead.
In each crack, a story breathes,
Whispers weave through autumn leaves.

Seconds linger, stretched so thin,
In the silence, worlds begin.
Whispered moments, lost and found,
In the cracks, solace abound.

A Piece of Whispering Chaos

In shadows dance the fleeting hues,
Whispers swirl like autumn's muse,
A chaotic breeze with stories told,
In sunswept glades, the heart feels bold.

Fingers trace the paths of night,
Stars collide in soft twilight,
Fragments of dreams begin to weave,
Cascades of thought in webs believe.

Echoes of laughter, lost and found,
The pulse of joy in quiet sound,
A world that spins, a vibrant hue,
In chaotic whispers, we break through.

Silence Woven in Fragments

In stillness sings the silent chord,
Words unspoken, barely heard,
Fragments of moments, woven tight,
Drifting softly into the night.

Tapestry of dreams unfold,
Stories spun, both new and old,
Echoes linger in the air,
Each hushed heartbeat, a gentle prayer.

Whispers float on the evening breeze,
In the quiet, the mind finds peace,
Woven threads of time and space,
In this silence, we find our place.

Time in Echoes

Ticking clocks in distant rooms,
Time whispers softly, gently looms,
Shadows stretch as minutes pass,
Memories reflected in the glass.

Echoes flutter on the walls,
Chronicles of ancient calls,
Every tick a tale retold,
In time's embrace, we find the bold.

A moment captured, held so near,
Time cascades, yet holds us dear,
In echoes of laughter and sighs,
We dance between the lows and highs.

A Shimmer of Broken Moonlight

Silver beams through tangled leaves,
Whispers weave where silence cleaves,
A shimmer caught in night's embrace,
Broken light finds its resting place.

Fragments of stars beneath the sky,
Echoes of wishes that dare to fly,
In the twilight, shadows blend,
Moonlit paths that never end.

Glimmers dance on the edge of dreams,
Woven together in silver streams,
Each broken ray a story told,
In moonlight's grasp, our hearts feel bold.

Fractured Silence

In the hush where shadows dwell,
Whispers chase the secret swell.
Time stands still, a breath held tight,
Echoes tremble in the night.

Forgotten dreams in corners creep,
Promises lost in fading sleep.
Silence stirs with tales untold,
Fragments glimmer, bright yet cold.

Winds carry sorrow's gentle plea,
Haunted sighs like drifting leaves.
Beneath the surface, ripples play,
Fractures dance in disarray.

Yet within the quiet's heart,
A spark ignites, a brand new start.
In the stillness, hope will bloom,
Turning shadows into room.

Echoes in the Void

In the vast, to nothing tied,
Thoughts like starlight slip and glide.
Whispers in the dark collide,
Seeking solace, nowhere hide.

Truths unfurl in cosmic dance,
Fleeting glimpses, an endless chance.
Time dissolves in muted sighs,
Echoes linger, no goodbyes.

A scream absorbed by endless night,
Fathomless depths absorb the light.
Mirrored worlds reflect the pain,
In the void, we start again.

Yet from silence, voices rise,
Lost creations touch the skies.
In the heartbeat, distant calls,
Hope ignites as darkness falls.

Stillness Unraveled

Amidst the chaos, silence waits,
Threads of calm in tangled fates.
Moments pause, then slip away,
Stillness whispers, come what may.

Through the noise, a songbird trills,
Softly weaving through the thrills.
In that hush, the world unfolds,
Like stories whispered, never told.

Crimson sunsets paint the sky,
Breathless hours, stillness sighs.
In the shadows, clarity gleams,
Unraveled webs, untapped dreams.

Beyond the rush, a gentle call,
Let emotions rise and fall.
In the calm, find what we seek,
Stillness speaks with colors meek.

When Calm Meets Chaos

When stormy skies begin to break,
Calm arises from the quake.
In the clash of dark and light,
Harmony shapes a new insight.

Turbulent winds weave through the trees,
Yet in the chaos, a soft breeze.
Racing hearts find steady ground,
In between, the peace is found.

Flashes strike, illuminating fate,
Moments bind, then hesitate.
A dance of forces, fierce and free,
At the edge of tranquility.

In this meld, the world aligns,
Chaos bows, serenity shines.
Together, they carve a way,
Uniting night and dawning day.

Chasing Shadows in Stillness

In twilight's grasp, shadows weave,
Moonlight's kiss, a subtle reprieve.
Silence dances on the breeze,
Time suspended, hearts at ease.

Footsteps echo on the grass,
Fleeting moments, none can last.
Chasing whispers lost in air,
Stillness cloaked in mystery's wear.

Stars unfold their silent tales,
Guiding dreams on gentle trails.
In the hush of night's embrace,
Shadows linger, a soft trace.

Awakened thoughts, they intertwine,
In stillness, all souls align.
Chasing shadows, finding light,
In the calm of endless night.

Whispers of a Torn Horizon

Through the clouds, a promise breaks,
Silent strength that stillness makes.
Horizon torn, yet hope ignites,
Whispers carried on winds of nights.

Fragments lost, yet beauty found,
In the chaos, stillness crowned.
Every thread, a story spun,
Voices echo, yet we're one.

Colors clash and shadows play,
Chasing dreams that lead astray.
But in the tear, we find our way,
Whispers guide us to the day.

In the distance, a light appears,
Mending hearts, erasing fears.
A horizon reborn once more,
In the whispers, we restore.

The Calm Before the Splinters

In velvet dusk, the silence grows,
A stillness deep, yet nobody knows.
The air is thick, a holding breath,
Calm prevails before the breadth.

Storms that gather just out of sight,
In shadows breathes a restless night.
Time fleeting, tensions bend,
Awaiting what the dawn will send.

Fragments poised on the edge of break,
In quiet, the stillness makes us ache.
Cracks appear beneath the skin,
The calm gives way, the splintered sin.

A watchful pause before the fall,
In silence, we prepare for all.
The heartbeats quicken, fears may splinter,
But in calm, we hold the winter.

Weavings of an Unquiet Mind

Threads of thought weave through the night,
An unquiet mind, no end in sight.
Patterns shift, then break apart,
In the tapestry, a restless heart.

Whispers of doubt, a constant hum,
Chasing echoes of what's to come.
Memories dance like flickering flames,
In webs of confusion, we play games.

Weaving hopes with strands of fear,
A fragile balance, year by year.
In the chaos, clarity hides,
An unquiet mind where mystery bides.

Yet in the fabric, dreams entwine,
Colors vibrant, life's design.
Though unquiet, we find our thread,
In the weavings of thoughts unsaid.

The Discord Among Starlit Silence

Under the sky, whispers collide,
Shadows twist in night's cold stride.
Stars tremble in a hidden refrain,
Harmony lost, replaced by pain.

Voices murmur through the dark,
Echoes linger, leaving a mark.
Cascades of light, they wane and splay,
Silent battles, night steals the day.

Orbs of color fade away,
While the heartache dares to stay.
In the void, dreams find their rest,
Discord reigns where once was blessed.

Yet in the twilight, hope will spark,
Faintly glowing within the dark.
Among the whispers, a soft plea,
To reclaim the night's lost harmony.

When the Calm Splinters

In the stillness, a crack appears,
Shattering peace, breeding fears.
Fragments scatter, silence breaks,
Every breath, a series of shakes.

Clouds gather, shadows fold,
A tale of chaos now retold.
Paths once clear turn into haze,
Calmness lost in sudden blaze.

Thoughts collide, emotions flare,
Finding solace becomes rare.
Ripples dance on shattered glass,
Time slips by, moments pass.

Yet amid the shattered peace,
Find the spark that will not cease.
Even in the trouble's grasp,
Hope entwines in fate's firm clasp.

Veins of Quiet Disarray

Threads of silence, tightly wound,
Within the noise, they lay profound.
Chaos hums a haunting tune,
Veins of quiet stretch by noon.

Streams of thought begin to clash,
In steady moments, shadows flash.
Fingers brush against the cold,
Hopes buried deep, yet to unfold.

A canvas smeared with shades of gray,
Fragments turn to disarray.
Yet in this mess, truths emerge,
Whispers born from quiet surge.

Hold the chaos, hold it tight,
In every sorrow, find the light.
Even when the world astray,
Beauty blooms in disarray.

Calm Before the Rupture

The air hangs heavy, tension builds,
As silent lull, anticipation yields.
Nature waits, breaths held in time,
Peace before the storm, so sublime.

Clouds gather, whispering dread,
A gentle hush where fear is fed.
Electric pulse beneath the skin,
The storm brews close, ready to begin.

Dark skies loom over distant hills,
A promise of chaos, nature spills.
Every heartbeat echoes loud,
Before the shatter, beneath the cloud.

But in that moment, watch and breathe,
Find solace strong in nature's weave.
For through the clash, purpose thrives,
In the calm, our spirit strives.

Fragments of Forgotten Peace

Whispers of time drift like leaves,
In shadows where silence weaves.
Moments lost in a gentle sigh,
Longing for the days gone by.

Echoes of laughter in the breeze,
Softly kissing the tall, swaying trees.
Beneath the sky, the memories dance,
In a dreamscape, a fleeting chance.

Cracks in the walls that hold the past,
Windows open, yet shadows cast.
Each fragment tells a tale untold,
In colors faded, but still bold.

When twilight falls and stars awaken,
A peace described, though often shaken.
In those fragments, a beauty creeps,
Restoring a soul that gently sleeps.

A Fragile Breath of Havoc

In the storm's eye, whispers collide,
A tempest born, destiny wide.
A fragile breath beneath the might,
Chaos dances in shades of light.

Every shadow, a story spun,
As worlds unravel, nowhere to run.
Tension crackles through the air,
Unseen forces, a hidden snare.

Flashes of truth in thunder's roar,
Promises whispered from distant shores.
Yet in the madness, a spark remains,
Flickering hope in stormy veins.

When silence reigns, the heart will race,
In fragile breaths, we find our place.
Havoc's lesson in every fight,
A tender shield, embracing night.

The Still That Cries

In quiet corners, shadows weep,
Beneath the weight of dreams they keep.
The stillness echoes a silent plea,
As ripples dance in memory's sea.

Frozen moments in the sun's last glare,
Subtle sighs linger in the air.
The heart beats softly, a muted plea,
For solace found in fragility.

Nature's cradle holds the broken,
Words unspoken, oh so laden.
In tender quiet, a sorrow's swell,
The still that cries, it knows us well.

Yet in the depths, a light may grow,
To guide lost spirits, soft and slow.
For even stillness, while it grieves,
Can bloom anew and mend what leaves.

Dissonance in Still Waters

Calm reflections mask the storm,
Beneath the surface, shadows swarm.
Ripples chatter, secrets spill,
In still waters, the heart remains still.

A paradox where silence reigns,
Yet within, a discord strains.
Time dances on with fleeting grace,
While chaos lingers in muted space.

Murmurs clash in the tranquil deep,
Stirring echoes that steal our sleep.
Dissonance blooms where peace should flow,
In the quiet depths, truths overflow.

Yet in the depths, we seek the spark,
A flicker of hope in shadows dark.
For even in dissonance, we find,
The beauty held within the mind.

Quietude in a Shattered Frame

In the dusk, whispers sway,
Fragments of a fading day.
Softly, shadows start to creep,
Lost in memories we once keep.

Quiet hush in corners, dim,
Echoes linger, soft and slim.
Cracks reveal a tale untold,
Beauty in the broken, bold.

Fleeting glimmers of the past,
In stillness, moments hold fast.
Silence blooms where chaos was,
A gentle sigh, a silent pause.

Through the glass, the world may flee,
Yet here, we find tranquility.
Embers glow, though shadows play,
In shattered frames, hope finds a way.

Crumbling Facades of Serenity

Beneath the surface, whispers fade,
Facade of calm, a masquerade.
Painted smiles, a fragile mask,
In stillness, truth, we dare to ask.

The garden blooms with tarnished grace,
Crumbling walls, time won't erase.
With every breath, we learn to see,
The strength in vulnerability.

Moments linger, gentle strife,
A dance between the dreams and life.
Softly we tread on scattered seeds,
From broken soil, new hope proceeds.

Fleeting tides of solace rise,
Beneath the weight, a heart replies.
In the cracks, we find our song,
In crumbling facades, we belong.

A Symphony of Unraveled Mends

Notes of silence gently play,
Threads of hope weave night and day.
Harmony in moments frayed,
A tapestry of dreams delayed.

Each fragment sings a different tune,
Echoes roam beneath the moon.
In disarray, we find our heart,
From tangled paths, we will not part.

Melodies in scattered light,
Unraveled seams bring forth the night.
In shadows, colors softly blend,
A symphony of hearts to mend.

As winds of change begin to blow,
Together, let our spirits grow.
In every note, resilience found,
Unraveled mends, a sacred sound.

The Stillness Before the Fall

Suspended breath in twilight's glow,
Time awaits, a cosmic show.
Horizon holds a breath of fate,
In stillness, destiny will wait.

Leaves quiver in silent grace,
Nature's heartbeat, a whispered space.
Anticipation throbs the air,
In the hush, we feel the rare.

Moments linger, poised to leap,
Secrets in the silence steep.
A gentle breeze, the world stands still,
In quietude, we feel the thrill.

From here, the leap will softly call,
In the stillness before the fall.
Embrace the calm, let troubles cease,
For in the pause, we find our peace.

Silence Beneath the Fracture

In the stillness where whispers fade,
Secrets linger in the shade.
Each crack a story left untold,
Silence wraps the night in gold.

Stars flicker like a distant cry,
Echoes of dreams that drift and die.
Beneath the surface, shadows crawl,
Silence reigns, it claims us all.

The Lament of Restless Shadows

Shadows dance on the creaking floor,
Yearning for a love they swore.
In their depths lies untamed fear,
Restless hearts that cannot steer.

Whispers float through dusky air,
Calling out for those who care.
But in the dark, they're lost and found,
In every sigh, a mournful sound.

Serenity's Tenuous Grip

A fragile peace upon the lake,
Reflections tremble, thoughts forsake.
In every ripple, a longing sigh,
Serenity whispers a tender lie.

Clouds drift slowly, a gentle tease,
Beneath, the heart begs for its ease.
Yet storms brew just beyond the rim,
And calm can vanish, swift and dim.

Broken Pieces of the Evening

Fragments scatter in twilight's gleam,
Each shard holds a fleeting dream.
The sun dips low, the horizon bleeds,
A canvas rich with scattered seeds.

Night cradles all that we hold dear,
In every crack, a voice we hear.
The broken pieces softly weep,
As evening wraps the world in sleep.

Jigsaw of the Inaudible

In shadows haunt the silent dreams,
Whispers float on fading beams,
Pieces lost in twilight's grasp,
A puzzle made to hide and clasp.

The echoes tie the world apart,
Fragments linger, beating heart,
Silent thoughts that twist and wind,
In every nook, the truth confined.

Patterns dance where none are seen,
Softly stitched, the quiet sheen,
Muffled words in the heavy air,
Connections formed, though rare and fair.

Reach for the void, a touch profound,
In the silence, secrets bound,
Each lost piece a story told,
In the inaudible, fate unfolds.

The Strain Beneath the Surface

Beneath the calm, a tempest brews,
Unseen currents, murky hues,
Veins of worry pulse like stars,
In oceans deep, with hidden scars.

The weight of words too heavy held,
In quiet rooms where dreams repelled,
Smiles disguise the flickering flame,
As all pretend, yet nothing's same.

Each silent cry, a paper-thin,
Layered heart, the ache within,
Beneath the smiles, the tears shall flow,
A hidden strain, we hardly show.

Yet strength can rise when hope's at stake,
In every breath, the chance we take,
To face the world, with courage bright,
And mend the seams that tear the light.

Quietude Ripped Asunder

In stillness lies the world awake,
A sudden shift, the calm does break,
Shattered echoes fill the air,
As silence crumbles, laid bare.

Fractured moments, wings unspooled,
The fragile peace that once was fooled,
Voices rise in sudden strife,
A haunting cry disturbs the life.

The quietude, once lush and green,
Now trembles 'neath a weight unseen,
Each whispered thought turns sharp and loud,
As chaos weaves its heavy shroud.

Yet from the wreckage, seeds may sprout,
In fractured past, we'll claim our route,
Through torn remains, new strength will grow,
And find again the peace we sow.

The Break of Solitude

In solitude, the heart does yearn,
For flickers bright, for love's return,
A quiet space where time stands still,
Yet whispers call beyond the hill.

The hours stretch like shadows long,
Within the silence, something's wrong,
Each thought a wave that swells and sways,
In lonely nights, we count the days.

But as the dawn brings light anew,
The break of dawn reveals the view,
Connections spark, a fleeting dance,
In chance encounters, hearts prance.

So solitude, though sweet and deep,
Can also lead to dreams we keep,
Embrace the chance, let shadows break,
For in the light, we find our wake.

The Lament of a Stilled Heart

In shadows where the memories dwell,
A heart once vibrant, now a shell.
The echoes of laughter fade away,
In silent rooms, lost dreams lay.

Each throbbing beat a distant sigh,
Underneath the endless sky.
Hope once flickered, now a spark,
In the depths, it feels so dark.

Time drips slowly, a cruel tease,
Fleeting moments, like autumn leaves.
Whispers haunt the quiet night,
Yearning for lost love's light.

Yet still the heart dares to ache,
In the stillness, memories wake.
For even stilled, it beats within,
A hope that love may start again.

Whispers Lost in the Fray

Amidst the chaos, voices blend,
A melody that seems to end.
Words like shadows slip away,
In tangled thoughts where we will stay.

Conversations drown in the noise,
In fleeting moments, we lose joys.
With every laugh, a truth concealed,
In silent battles, hearts are healed.

The world spins on, but we are caught,
In whispers shared, but soon forgot.
Threads of stories weave and fray,
Hold on tight, don't drift away.

In the fray, we find our place,
Searching for a familiar face.
Though whispers fade and voices strain,
In shared silence, love remains.

The Broken Silence Speaks

In the corners where shadows dwell,
The silence broken, tales to tell.
Voices linger in the air,
Echoes of a love laid bare.

Each sigh a story, softly penned,
In the quiet, hearts can mend.
What was lost now finds its way,
In the stillness of the day.

Words unspoken, yet they fall,
In broken moments, we hear the call.
Fragments of a deeper theme,
Awakened from a fleeting dream.

Through the silence, truths arise,
Revealed beneath the evening skies.
The broken silence tells our tale,
In whispers soft, we shall prevail.

Moments Dispersed like Glass

Shattered dreams upon the floor,
Each fragment a memory, nothing more.
Moments caught in fragile light,
Dancing softly, taking flight.

Reflections of what used to be,
Glimmers of laughter, joy so free.
Yet time, like shadows, fades away,
Leaving traces of yesterday.

We grasp at shards, so sharp, so bright,
Holding on with all our might.
In every piece, a story lies,
Of moments lost, beneath the skies.

Though scattered wide, we still embrace,
The beauty found in every place.
Moments, like glass, may break apart,
But in our souls, they hold a heart.

Threads of Eclipsed Harmony

In shadows where the silence weaves,
A melody of whispers grieves.
Each note, a thread of twilight spun,
In the dark, our songs undone.

Fingers trace the fading light,
Beneath the cloak of endless night.
Yet in the hush, a hope will bloom,
In fractured tunes, we find our room.

Voices woven, soft and rare,
In hidden corners, hearts laid bare.
Together we embrace the fray,
In the echoes, lost, we stay.

Through the seams of time, we glide,
Where harmony and silence bide.
In the dance of dusk we find
Threads of peace that gently bind.

The Shattered Glass of Now

Reflections shattered on the floor,
Fragments of what we once adored.
Time forgets its gentle caress,
Leaving us in this emptiness.

Each jagged piece tells stories past,
Of fleeting moments that never last.
We gather shards, the hurt, the thrill,
Wounds we nurse, yet can't fulfill.

In the chaos, we find our way,
Through glimmers of a brighter day.
Yet shadows linger, haunting still,
In shards of glass, we seek our will.

As we sift through the broken dreams,
In silent nights, the moonlight gleams.
Together we'll reflect and mend,
The shattered glass can still transcend.

A Still Heart in the Storm

Beneath the tempest's raging roar,
A quiet pulse, a whispered lore.
In chaos, calm begins to rise,
Amidst the howling, silent cries.

Waves crash hard against the shore,
Yet in my chest, the stillness soars.
The storm may bend, but I stand tall,
A sturdy tree when shadows call.

Breath of wind and rain collide,
Yet here I find my strength inside.
Roots run deep, and branches sway,
In nature's rage, I learn to stay.

For even storms must pass in time,
And through the tempest, hearts can climb.
A still heart beats, unyielding, bold,
In storms that whisper tales untold.

Echoing Dreams and Dismay

In the stillness where dreams collide,
Faint echoes beckon from the tide.
Whispers linger in the air,
Of hopes that fade, of love and care.

A shadow dances on the wall,
Fleeting visions of rise and fall.
In corridors where silence stays,
We wander lost in endless maze.

Dismay clings like a heavy fog,
Ensnaring hearts in its thick smog.
Yet dreams ignite the darkest night,
A flicker, small, a guiding light.

In the echo, we find our song,
A melody to carry on.
Through tangled thoughts we'll make our way,
In echoing dreams, we shall not sway.

Fragments of Forgotten Peace

In shadows where silence breathes,
A whisper of hope barely weaves.
Time carries the scars of our past,
Fleeting moments, too fragile to last.

Through twilight, a glimmer of grace,
A flicker in an infinite space.
Memories, like petals, softly fall,
Dancing gently, responding to a call.

The echo of laughter fades away,
As the sun bids farewell to the day.
Yet in the stillness, hearts still yearn,
For the peace we hope to return.

In fragments, we gather our dreams,
A tapestry woven of silent screams.
Though broken, our spirits remain,
Searching for solace through the pain.

Veils of Disrupted Harmony

A song once sweet now turns to ash,
Notes lost in a thunderous crash.
Veils flutter in a chaotic breeze,
Whispers of love that never please.

Calm waters churn under dark skies,
Where once were stars, now only sighs.
Echoes of laughter turned to sound,
A symphony broken, lost underground.

In the heart, a cavern of discord,
Where melodies fade, dreams are ignored.
Yet hope lingers, like a distant drum,
Waiting for harmony to again come.

Amidst the noise, a silent plea,
For the return of tranquility.
Though veils may hide what we can't see,
In the stillness, we'll find our key.

The Sound of Shattered Dreams

Crimson skies and the edge of night,
Lost aspirations fade from sight.
Whispers drift through the empty air,
Stories untold, a silent despair.

In the chambers of the restless heart,
Hope flickers like a dying spark.
The echoes of joy now taut with fear,
Remnants of dreams that once drew near.

Fragments echo, a haunting refrain,
A melody wrapped in invisible chains.
We chase shadows in a desperate race,
Searching for solace in this vast space.

Yet among the ruins, light may break,
A chance to mend, a vow to make.
From shattered dreams, new paths appear,
Transforming silence, erasing fear.

Breach in the Muffled Air

In quiet corners, secrets hide,
Silent wonders that can't abide.
A breach of stillness speaks aloud,
Stories unfold, though wrapped in cloud.

Breath held tight in the broken night,
Every whisper turns to fright.
Echoes of truths we dare not share,
Rising softly in the soft, thick air.

With every heartbeat, tension grows,
A yearning that only the silence knows.
We search for a hand, a gentle touch,
To heal the wounds that hurt so much.

But hope glimmers through the heavy shroud,
Promising peace in the bustling crowd.
As breeches mend and fears decline,
We'll find our way, hearts intertwined.

The Fractured Veil of Peace

A whisper lost within the night,
Promises fade beyond the light,
Dreams unwind like fragile thread,
As silence wraps the world in dread.

Fleeting moments slip away,
Shadows dance where children play,
Innocence drifts like fallen leaves,
Hope, it seems, is what deceives.

Beneath the calm, the storm does brew,
What once was clear now feels askew,
The fractured veil, a burdened seam,
Cracks reveal a broken dream.

Yet in the twilight's gentle glow,
A seed of peace begins to grow,
Through shattered fragments, hearts will mend,
In pain, we find a way to bend.

Shards of the Unheard

Echoes linger in the air,
Words unspoken, filled with care,
Jumbled thoughts begin to sway,
In silence, truths are kept at bay.

Voices drown in endless plight,
Fear and doubt consume the night,
Every shard of what we feel,
Crafts a wound and can't conceal.

Hidden stories yearn to shine,
Captured moments, lost in time,
With every whisper veiled in pain,
Unheard songs of dark remain.

Yet through the gloom, a glimmer glows,
The heart persists, the courage grows,
Shards may cut, but they can heal,
As we learn the weight of real.

A Stillness Forgotten

In crowded streets where ghosts once roamed,
A silent pulse, we feel alone,
Time stands still, a fleeting chance,
Where echoes of the past do dance.

The muted world, a heavy sigh,
Chasing shadows, asking why,
Faint memories in dusty frames,
Crumble softly, lose their names.

Moments yearn for hands to hold,
In the stillness, stories told,
Yet hearts remember, even if lost,
The warmth of presence, worth the cost.

From silence grows a fragile sound,
In forgotten stillness, hope is found,
A chance to breathe, to start anew,
In every pause, the world breaks through.

Disrupted Lullabies

Softly sung through weary nights,
A melody of fleeting sights,
Yet waking dreams, they drift away,
Leaving only shadows gray.

Each note a thread, a comfort near,
Now tangled whispers filled with fear,
The lullabies of old now churn,
As restless hearts await their turn.

In the dawn, where peace should reign,
Lies the weight of unresolved pain,
Hushed were the hopes that once took flight,
Lost in depths of endless night.

Still, we sing through tears that blind,
Finding solace, the heart is kind,
Through disrupted songs, a spark survives,
In every echo, love derives.

Uneasy Winds of Change

The leaves dance wildly in the breeze,
Whispers of change in the rustling trees.
Footsteps hesitated, where paths collide,
What once felt certain, now must decide.

Clouds gather darkly, shadows take flight,
Tales of tomorrow weave through the night.
Hearts clutch the past, afraid to explore,
Yet beyond the storm, lies an open door.

Threads of Disrupted Dreams

Stitches unravel in the moonlit seam,
Fading reflections of a once bright dream.
Whispers of hope float, frayed at the edge,
Tethered to moments, we dare to hedge.

Beneath the surface, the currents churn,
Lessons forgotten, yet still we learn.
Fragments of wishes scatter like dust,
In the quiet darkness, we place our trust.

Conversations in Fractured Light

Flickers of laughter in the broken glow,
Shadows entwined in the tales they throw.
Eyes speak volumes in the silence between,
Words left unspoken paint shades so keen.

The dance of dialogue, missteps and grace,
Finding connection in the fleeting space.
Fingers brush lightly, the moment ignites,
In crooked reflections, the world ignites.

Fray of Tranquil Shadows

Soft whispers echo in the twilight air,
A lullaby woven with tender care.
Beneath the surface, a ripple of peace,
Yet hidden turmoil fails to cease.

Trees stand watchful, their secrets concealed,
In the realm of quiet, emotions revealed.
The heart knows solace but yearns for the storm,
In the fray of shadows, we dance to stay warm.

Fractured Whispers in Still Night

Beneath the stars, shadows creep,
Secrets stutter, too deep.
Sighs dance softly through the air,
Fractured whispers, dreams laid bare.

Moonlight bathes the silent ground,
In the stillness, hearts resound.
Fading echoes haunt the breeze,
In the night, the spirits tease.

Lullabies in tones of gray,
Floating memories drift away.
Tales of love, now out of reach,
Fractured whispers, time can preach.

When dawn breaks, silence reigns,
Yet in the heart, the whisper remains.
In every shadow, past resides,
Fractured whispers, where hope abides.

Collapsed Dreams

Beneath the weight of endless sighs,
Lie the echoes of our cries.
Shattered visions, hopes once bright,
Now scattered in the fading light.

Pages torn from future's book,
Each one tells a story's nook.
Fractured realms where wishes dwelled,
In silent screams, the heart is held.

Fleeting glimpses of what could be,
Lost within the maze of memory.
Chasing shadows, running fast,
Collapsed dreams, shadows cast.

In the quiet of a midnight tear,
Wisps of yearning linger near.
Yet hope can rise from ashes gray,
From collapsed dreams, a brand new day.

Threads of Silence Unspooled

In the tapestry of night,
Threads of silence weave their light.
Whispered thoughts, a gentle theme,
Life entwined in a fragile dream.

Crimson stains on memory's page,
Time unravels, hearts engage.
Loose connections, frayed and bare,
In the stillness, a secret dare.

Hands that touch but never meet,
Echoes carried on the street.
Each moment slips through hesitant hands,
Threads of silence, vast and grand.

Beneath the dark, a yearning stands,
Stories whispered in scattered strands.
In the quiet, faith may fuel,
Threads of silence, softly cruel.

Longing in Quiet Ruins

Amidst the rubble, silence reigns,
Void of laughter, void of chains.
Time-worn stones bear witness still,
Longing echoes, deep as a well.

Forgotten dreams, dust-covered tales,
In the shadows, sorrow prevails.
Memories linger, bittersweet,
Longing pulse beneath the beat.

Overgrown paths lead the way,
To remnants of a brighter day.
Where hope once bloomed, now just remains,
Longing whispered through love's veins.

Yet in the dusk, a spark will rise,
From quiet ruins, hear the cries.
For in the heart, a seed takes hold,
Longing breathes, and dreams unfold.

In The Wake of Silent Fractures

Whispers of time, they linger slow,
In places where shadows quietly grow.
Each crack in the earth, a tale untold,
Of dreams once bright, now faded gold.

Rustling leaves bear witness to pain,
As silence drapes like a soft refrain.
The weight of the world, a heavy shroud,
Hiding the echoes beneath the crowd.

Yet hope seeps through the silent cracks,
Reviving the warmth that time lacks.
With every breath, we learn to mend,
In the wake of fractures, paths can bend.

Embrace the rawness of what we bleed,
For even in sorrow, there's room to lead.
In solace found among strange roots,
Lie the seeds of a life that still fruits.

Beauty in the Chaos of Stillness

In moments where stillness greets the night,
Chaos unfolds, yet feels so right.
Whispers of dreams glide softly past,
In the quiet, the shadows are cast.

Time bows low with a gentle sigh,
As stars awaken in the blanket sky.
Beauty unfurls with every chance,
In the chaos, we find our dance.

Nature's brush paints in shades of grace,
Creating warmth in this sacred space.
In each flutter of leaves, a spark ignites,
Turning silence into vibrant flights.

Let the heart resonate with each breath,
Finding life in the quiet's depth.
For chaos and stillness together weave,
A tapestry rich, in which we believe.

Torn Pages of a Silent Story

In the corner lies an unwritten tale,
Fragments of thoughts, a fragile hail.
Pages once filled with laughter and tears,
Now scattered like dreams, lost through years.

Ink bleeds softly where memories fade,
A silent story that time has made.
Each torn page whispers of what could be,
In the echoes of silence, we learn to see.

Resilience grows from the shreds of pain,
Finding beauty in what remains.
In the heart of the broken, hope may shine,
Writing anew, stories intertwine.

Let every scrap gather and mend,
For the silent story is not the end.
In these fragments, we find our way,
Creating new chapters from yesterday.

The Stillness Beneath the Shredded Sky

Beneath the canvas ripped and torn,
Lies a stillness quiet and worn.
Clouds may clash with thunderous cries,
Yet peace whispers where silence lies.

Amongst the debris of dreams long past,
Hope flickers softly, steadfast.
In the chaos of storms that rage and shout,
The heart learns what love is about.

Stars still shine in the midst of grief,
Carving out spaces, granting relief.
For even when skies appear so bleak,
The stillness rests, quiet and meek.

In the echoes of thunder, we find our voice,
A reminder of strength, in sorrow, rejoice.
For beneath the shredded sky's wild call,
Lies a stillness that nurtures us all.

The Quiet Cascade

Water flows with a gentle sigh,
Over stones that quietly lie.
Moments drip in a soft refrain,
Nature's whispers, a sweet refrain.

Trees lean close, to hear the song,
Of the cascade, where they belong.
Sunlight dances on rippling waves,
In this haven, the spirit braves.

Time stands still, as shadows play,
Chasing dreams that drift away.
Echoes linger, soft and light,
In the glow of fading night.

Here beneath the vast expanse,
Life unfolds in a quiet dance.
The cascade calls, a soothing sound,
In this peace, the heart is found.

Whispers Through Torn Pages

Old words flutter like silent birds,
Carried forth on the breeze's words.
Tattered tales, in shadows hide,
Whispers where forgotten dreams bide.

Ink faded, yet stories remain,
Echoing softly through joy and pain.
Each line a thread, woven tight,
Binding time within the night.

Pages turn with a gentle sigh,
Hidden secrets that never die.
Memory lingers, soft and warm,
In the silence, a quiet storm.

Through the cracks, winds gently weave,
Stories lost, yet we still believe.
In the heart, they find a place,
Torn pages, a sweet embrace.

The Echo of Unraveling Thoughts

In the mind, a dance of ideas,
Fleeting visions like autumn leaves.
Thoughts collide in a swirling haze,
Each echo leads through tangled maze.

Fragments pulse like a soft heartbeat,
Searching for patterns, calm and sweet.
Words drift like clouds on a breeze,
Hoping to settle, drift, and seize.

Silence beckons, a gentle guide,
Unraveling whispers, deep inside.
In quiet moments, truth unfolds,
A tapestry of stories told.

As dawn breaks, clarity shines bright,
Chasing shadows, igniting light.
In the echo of thoughts laid bare,
Freedom breathes in the crisp air.

Reflections in a Broken Mirror

Shattered glass reflects the past,
Fragments holding memories cast.
Each piece a story, sharp and clear,
Whispers of dreams, lost and near.

In broken edges, beauty lies,
Glimmers of hope beneath the sighs.
A patchwork portrait, torn and true,
With splintered paths, the light breaks through.

Dancing shadows, a haunting dance,
Twisting through each fractured glance.
What once was whole now finds its way,
In jagged lines, bright hues display.

Yet in the cracks, a glow persists,
Reflections of love, and sunlit trysts.
In every shard, a truth to wear,
Life's broken beauty—a silent prayer.

Shattered Reflections of what Was

In glassy shards, the memories lie,
Fragments of laughter, a soft goodbye.
What once was whole, now scattered around,
In silence, the echoes of dreams profound.

Faded whispers dance in the air,
Haunting reminders of feelings laid bare.
Time drifts on, like a river's flow,
Carrying pieces of all we let go.

Each shard a story, both bitter and sweet,
In darkness and light, the past feels complete.
Yet here in the fragments, I search for a sign,
Of what it once meant, of love so divine.

Shadows linger, where sunlight used to gleam,
A tapestry woven from hopes and dreams.
In broken reflections, I find my way back,
To the essence of us, though the colors lack.

The Echo of a Breathless Pause.

In the stillness, a heartbeat stops,
A moment suspended, where breath lightly drops.
Time holds its breath, in softest embrace,
Echoes of silence carve out a space.

Fleeting thoughts drift like snowflakes in air,
Each one a whisper that lingers to share.
In the hush of the night, shadows silently play,
Tracing the outlines of words left to say.

The weight of the world feels lighter, yet dense,
In the pause, there's a softness, an unexplained sense.
A glance exchanged speaks more than a word,
In the echo of stillness, the truth is inferred.

Breathlessly caught in a dance of the soul,
Moments like these make us feel deeply whole.
In every fraction of time, we truly belong,
The echo of silence teaches us strong.

Fractured Echoes

Cracks in the surface reveal hidden tales,
Fractured echoes ride on the wind's gales.
What once was clear now shimmers in doubt,
In each broken whisper, our truths pour out.

Shadows flutter, like butterflies lost,
Weight of regret brings us down at a cost.
In the spaces in between, we search for the light,
A glimpse of connection in the long, lonely night.

Mirror reflections, a jigsaw undone,
Pieces scattered, yet they still seek the sun.
Every shattered moment, a lesson we find,
In the heart of the chaos, beauty intertwined.

Yet in this fracture, hope softly grows,
Tendrils of courage through darkness it sows.
From echoes of sorrow, new voices will rise,
A symphony crafted as the old voice sighs.

Whispered Fragments

Whispers float gently on the edge of the night,
Fragments of memories, soft and light.
In the quiet, our secrets weave dreams,
Dancing in shadows, as hope softly gleams.

Each fragment a story, a piece of the heart,
Scattered like stars, each plays a part.
In the silence of moments, our truths come alive,
In whispered breaths, our spirits survive.

Through veils of the past, we find a way through,
In the hush of the night, love sings warm and true.
Here in the fragments, the soul learns to mend,
In whispered confessions, we find our own blend.

So gather the whispers, the fragments of light,
Each one a promise that shines in the night.
Together they form a tapestry bright,
In whispered fragments, our hearts take flight.

Shattered Reflections of the Soul

In shards of silver, memories gleam,
Lost in the void, like a fleeting dream.
Each piece a whisper, a story untold,
Fragments of warmth in the bitter cold.

Mirror, mirror, fractured and bare,
Echoes of laughter, woven in air.
Locked in the glass, past shadows reside,
Shattered reflections where hopes collide.

The heart too heavy, the weight unknown,
In the silence, fears have grown.
Yet through the cracks, light seeps through,
Beautiful chaos, in shades of blue.

Mending the edges, one spark at a time,
Finding the rhythm, reclaiming the rhyme.
Though broken and bruised, the soul will prevail,
Through shattered reflections, we learn to set sail.

Echoes in the Still Air

Whispers of winds weave through the trees,
Soft as the dusk, a gentle breeze.
Carrying tales of the day's sweet sighs,
Echoes of laughter beneath painted skies.

Moments linger, suspended in time,
A distant chime, a heart's soft rhyme.
Silence wraps softly around each sound,
In this still air, our dreams are unbound.

Sipping on twilight, a fragrant embrace,
Holding the stillness in quiet grace.
With every breath, the world finds its way,
Into the night, where shadows play.

Echoes remain like a tender kiss,
In the still air, we find our bliss.
For in the silence, we learn to see,
The beauty that lives in our memory.

Ruins of Restful Moments

In quiet corners, the past lies still,
Ruins of moments that time cannot kill.
Gentle the echoes that linger about,
Soft as the dawn, where whispers break out.

Fragments of laughter, scattered like leaves,
Entwined with the scent of memories it weaves.
A tapestry rich, worn by the years,
Crafted in joy, stitched with our tears.

Beneath the rubble, a heartbeat resides,
In the ruins, where nostalgia abides.
Finding our peace in the remnants below,
Taking our time, letting the stillness grow.

As night descends, the shadows will play,
Over the ruins, in gentle array.
Restful the moments, though faded they seem,
In every fragment, we're living the dream.

Splintered Calm

A stillness shattered by the heart's own strife,
In splintered calm, we seek out life.
Cracks in the silence, echoes collide,
Underneath the stillness, where sentiments hide.

Glistening twilight paints shadows anew,
Where vibrant colors emerge from the blue.
In moments of peace, the fragments descend,
An artful dance where soft textures blend.

Holding the quiet, yet chaos prevails,
In every breath, the tempest regales.
Yet in these splinters, we find our grace,
Calm like a river, in time and space.

For even in turmoil, the heart finds a way,
Through splintered calm, we learn to stay.
Amidst the shards lies the truth's embrace,
In fractured stillness, we carve out our place.

Milton Keynes UK
Ingram Content Group UK Ltd.
UKHW031319271124
451618UK00007B/231